NEW

# The wind and the sun

## and other stories

**The wind and the sun**   page 2

**The boy who cried wolf**   page 10

**The wind, the rain and the sparrow**   page 17

Nelson

# The wind and the sun

The wind and the sun were talking
one day.
They saw a man walking along
wearing a big coat.
I can make him take his coat off
before you can, said the wind.

The sun looked at the wind.
Do you think so? said the sun.
Yes, said the wind.
I can make him take his coat off
before you can.
Show me, said the sun.

The wind began to blow.
The wind went whoosh,
down on to the man's head.
The wind went whoosh,
under the man's coat.
But the man did not take off his coat.

The wind blew more and more.
Leaves were blown down from the trees.
They danced along the road.
Still the man did not take off his coat.

The wind gave up at last.
That man will never take his coat off,
said the wind.
I could blow and blow all day long and
he would still keep it on.

I can make him take his coat off,
said the sun.
How can you do that? asked the wind.
Just you wait and see, said the sun and
he smiled a sunny smile.

The sun began to shine down on the man.

The man began to smile.

He looked up at the sun.

The sun shone more and more.

The man smiled more and more.

The man began to feel very hot in
his big coat, so he took it off.
I was kind to the man, said the sun.
That is how to get things done.

# The boy who cried wolf

Once there was a boy who looked after
the sheep up in the hills.
One day he said to himself,
I will play a trick on the people.
So he shouted, Wolf. Wolf.

All the people ran up the hill.
They shouted and clapped their hands
to make the wolf run away.
They were cross when they saw
there was no wolf.
The boy just laughed at them.

Some days later, the boy shouted again.
Wolf. Wolf, he cried.
The people ran up the hill again.
They were very cross when
they saw there was no wolf.
The boy just laughed at them.

After a few more days,
the boy shouted again.
Wolf. Wolf, he cried.
Once more the people ran up the hill.
This time they were very, very cross.
The boy just laughed at them.

Then one day a wolf did come.
The boy ran away and
shouted, Wolf. Wolf.
But this time no one came.
That silly boy is playing
his tricks again, the people said.
We will not answer.

The wolf killed all the sheep.
The boy hid behind a rock until
the wolf had gone.
Then he ran all the way home
as fast as he could.

The boy had tricked the people
too many times.
If you tell lies like this boy,
then no one will believe you
when you do tell the truth.

# The wind, the rain and the sparrow

The wind and the rain and the sun
went out to play.
They played in the Red Indians' camp.
I can blow down their blankets,
said the wind. I can blow
their fires and their feathers.
This is great fun, said the wind.

The Indians were not happy.
We must ask the sun to help us,
said the Big Chief.
Please tell the wind to stop,
the Big Chief said to the sun.
The sun called the wind.
You will have to go away if
you can't stop, said the sun.
It was only fun, said the wind.

Just then the wind blew down
the Indians' tents.
The sun was angry.
Go away wind and don't come back until
you can be good, said the sun.
I'll go away, said the wind.
I'll go away too, said the rain.
We won't come back, they said.

Thank you sun, said the Big Chief.
The sun shone and shone and
everyone was happy.
Then one day, the Big Chief said,
I am hot. I need some water.
We have no water. said the Indians.
The wind has gone and
the rain has gone too.
There is no water in our wells.

We must ask the sun to help us,
said the Big Chief.
We are hungry and thirsty.
We have no food and no water and
our crops have died.
Please ask the rain to come back.

The sun called the wind and the rain,
but they did not come back.
They were afraid so they hid in a cave.
What shall we do? said the Big Chief.
I can help, said the little sparrow.
I will fly with a feather in my mouth.
The wind will blow the feather,
so we will find them.
Good, said the sun.

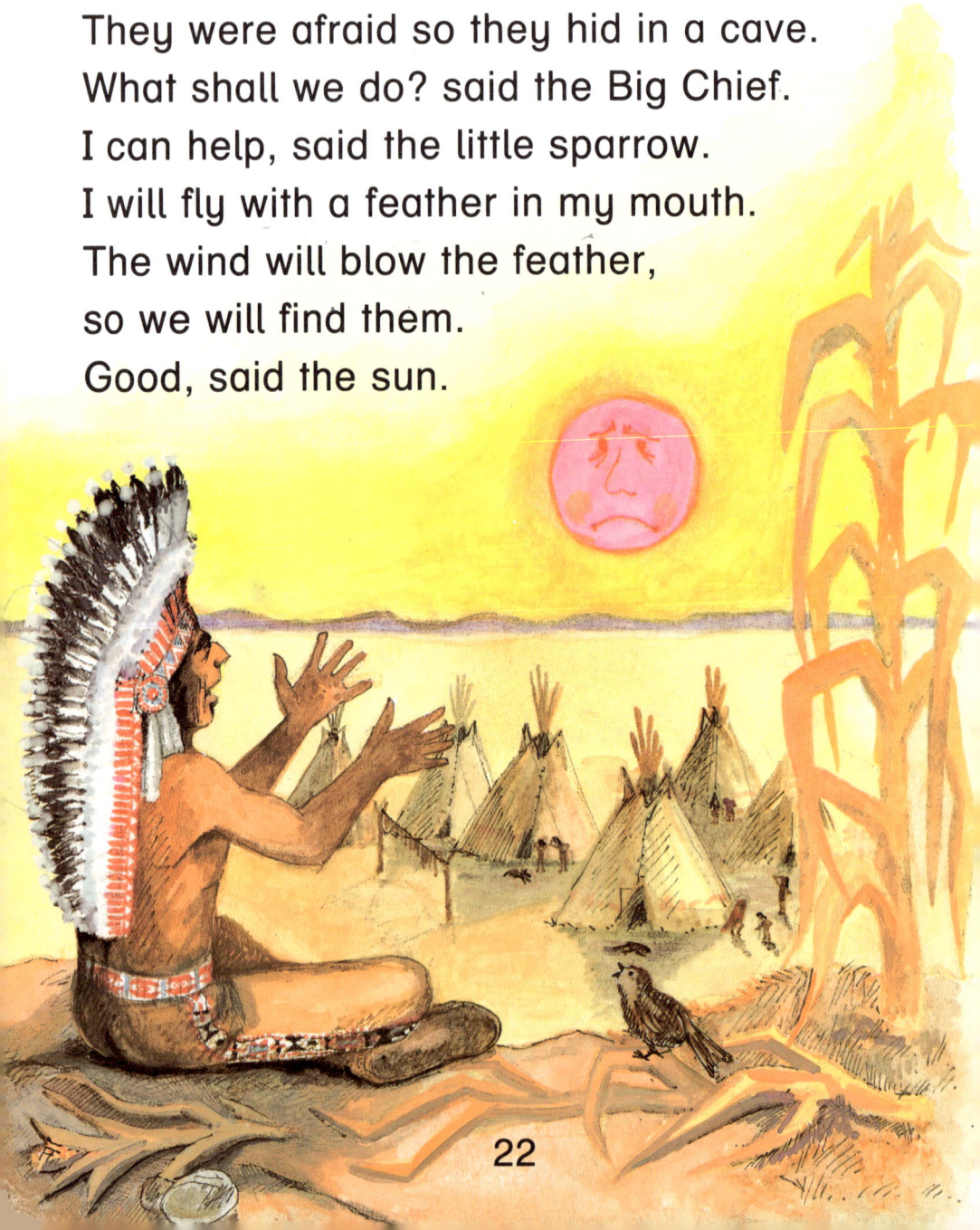

So the sparrow flew off.
He flew here and he flew there and
as he flew he sang,
Come out wind. Come out rain.
We all want you back again.
Suddenly the feather blew out of
the little sparrow's mouth.
The wind and the rain came out
of their cave.

The Indians felt the wind on their faces
and they smiled at the wind.
The rain came and filled the wells with
water and the crops began to grow.
The sun was happy and the wind
was happy and the rain was happy.
But most of all, the Indians were happy.